GW01246755

LOOKING GOOD FEELING GREAT

Susan Martineau and Lone Morton
Illustrated by Louise Comfort
Comic strip by Bob Harvey

INTRODUCTION

HI THERE! MY NAME IS BETH. I LOVE ALL PETS, SWIMMING AND MOST SPORT. MY BEST FRIENDS ARE JENNY AND ROS.

MY FAVE THING IS READING.

I THINK HATS ARE BRILL! I WANT TO BE A FASHION DESIGNER.

WE ALL THINK THIS BOOK HAS SOME FAB IDEAS. I HOPE YOU DO TOO!

WOW, LOOK AT THAT LIST. THERE'S EVEN SOME YOGA. COR, I'M NOT STANDING ON ONE LEG!

CONTENTS

1
NATURAL GOOD LOOKS

Jenny's feeling blue —

MY MUM SAYS I'VE GOT TO HAVE MY HAIR CUT IF I DON'T KEEP IT OUT OF MY EYES.

Later —

THANKS, ROS. I REALLY LIKE THE FRENCH PLAIT... I'M GOING TO PRACTISE DOING IT MYSELF.

Beth tries another style —

MM ...I'M NOT SURE THIS STYLE'S REALLY ME!

Later —

OH NO! WHAT A GROSS SMELL!

DO YOU THINK WE'VE GOT THE RIGHT INGREDIENTS FOR THE HAIR CONDITIONER, BETH?

YEAH — GO ON GIVE IT ANOTHER STIR!

THIS IS BRILLIANT!

BUT I'M NOT SURE WHAT MUM'LL SAY ABOUT THE KITCHEN ...

Next day before school —

AAAH! I FOUND A SPOT THIS MORNING!

Later at school —

OK I GUESS NOT — BUT WHAT DOES THE BOOK SAY?

DON'T PANIC ROS — IT'S NOT AN EMERGENCY.

Read on —

HAIR

Changing your hairstyle can really make you feel good. Have fun trying new hairstyles. Go to a hairdresser or ask a grown-up if you want a cut. It's best not to do-it-yourself with the scissors!

How to plait

Divide hair into 3 strands.

Plait right-hand strand over middle.

Plait left-hand strand over the middle strand. Continue and fasten at bottom.

Plait your hair all over while it's still damp. Dry gently. ➔

Undo the plaits and fluff out with your dryer.

◄ Weave a scarf or ribbon into the plait.

Use a covered elastic to fasten plaits and pony-tails. An ordinary elastic band will damage your hair.

Wacky waves

No need for a hairdresser to create this glamour look. Works with medium or long hair.

For a party, spray colour on one strand. (Make sure it can be washed off easily!)

HAIR TIP
The ends of your hair can dry and split. So have your hair trimmed regularly and it'll look and feel much better.

Short and funky

Use gel to tame wisps – or give yourself a spiky look. Brighten up a party with super sparkling gel!

HAIR QUIZ
True or false?

1 Your hair grows faster in summer.
2 You shed all your old hair in the winter months.
3 Head lice prefer clean hair.
4 Cutting hair strengthens it.

(Answers on inside back cover)

Hot hairdryers can damage hair. Use the low temperature and shake hair with your hand or use a diffuser.

FRENCH PLAIT

Plaiting is easier to do if your hair hasn't just been washed.

Finish off with a normal plait plus covered elastic or a scrunchie (see p.7).

How to do a French plait
Ask someone to help you at first. Practice makes perfect!

Gather handful of hair at top of head. Divide into 3 and do one normal plait.

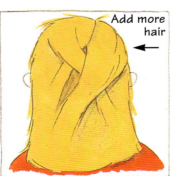

Add more hair →

Next take some hair from side of head and add to right-hand strand. Plait it over middle strand. Keep strands tight and neat.

Add more hair →

Then add hair to left strand. Plait over middle one. Continue adding and plaiting.

A cool style for you?

Brush well before starting.
It's sometimes easier to style hair
that's damp.

FUNKY PLAITS

← Start each with a
ponytail. Divide
into 3 strands,
twist right strand
to the right several
times and cross
over the other 2.
Keep twisting and
crossing over each
right-hand strand.

Make as many plaits
as you like.

Always losing your
pencil? Here's a safe
place to keep it!

DOUBLE PONYTAIL

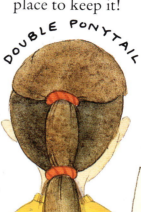

HIGH PONYTAIL

 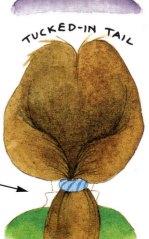

PARTING TIP
Draw a comb down
the scalp where you
want a parting.

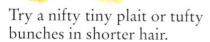

Try a nifty tiny plait or tufty
bunches in shorter hair.

Twist a ponytail and
coil it round – fix
with pins or even
chopsticks!

BALLET BUN

Finish off plaits
and bunches
with ribbons,
jazzy shoelaces
and snazzy clips.

Make a ponytail.
Between head and
fastening open a gap
and feed ponytail
through. Pull down.

TUCKED-IN TAIL

Hair bits

You don't need to spend loads of money to have brilliant bits to put in your hair. Even making a scrunchie is dead easy!

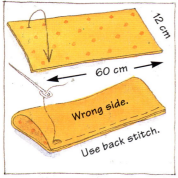

60 cm
12 cm
Wrong side.
Use back stitch.

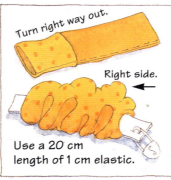

Turn right way out.
Right side.
Use a 20 cm length of 1 cm elastic.

Decorate with sequins or stitches.
Join and sew.

Cut flimsy fabric or scrap to size. Fold. Sew edge (see p.14).

Turn tube inside out – right side out. Use safety-pin to thread elastic through tube.

Tie elastic ends tightly. Join fabric ends, turn under to neaten and sew together. Decorate.

Alice band
Before decorating, wrap ribbon tightly round it and secure at end.

Stretchy band

Make a fab and smart hairband by dressing up a basic band with beads, buttons, bobbles and badges.

Make a snazzy clip by gluing small toys, balloons, bobbles, bows to a basic hairclip.

FUN FACTS
The average scalp has over a million hairs growing on it. The longest hair ever recorded is 365 cm!

Hair care

Your hair needs care to keep it looking good but you don't need to buy expensive potions. Try a herbal rinse for extra shine.

WASHING TIPS
- Brush your hair before washing it.
- Always make sure all the shampoo is well rinsed out.
- After swimming always wash your hair.

A beaten egg yolk combed into hair and left for 20 minutes is a magic conditioner. Rinse well though!

FUN FACT
The record for splitting one human hair is 17 times!

HERBAL TIP
You could always grow your own in pots or in the garden.

To make a herbal rinse

Take a few fresh sprigs or a herbal teabag of your chosen herb and place in a jug. Pour on boiling water, let it cool and use as final rinsing water.

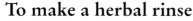

CAMOMILE FOR FAIR HAIR

ROSEMARY FOR DARK

MARIGOLD FOR RED

PARSLEY FOR DANDRUFF!

SKIN

For healthy skin, drink lots of water, eat plenty of yummy fresh fruit and vegetables and get lots of sleep.

At Beth's house —

KEEP STILL, OR IT'LL GO IN YOUR EYES!

I RECKON I'VE GOT TO KEEP THESE ON FOR ABOUT 15 MINUTES.

IT LOOKS GROSS BUT FEELS GREAT.

Cucumber face pack

- 2-3 slices of peeled cucumber
- 2 teaspoons of thick plain yoghurt
- ¼ teaspoon of lemon juice

Mash the cucumber and mix with yoghurt and lemon juice.

Spread evenly, avoiding eyes and mouth. Protect clothes with towel. Leave on for 15 minutes. Rinse off.

Cool eyes

Place a slice of cucumber on each eye and lie back to listen to your fave band!

SKIN FACTS

1 House dust is mostly made up of dead skin flakes!
2 Skin is covered with very fine hairs to protect it and keep it warm.
3 Skin colour depends on the amount of melanin in it – this is a substance which protects skin from the sun.

TAKE CARE!

If any lotions or potions make your skin sore or red, don't use them.

Bath herbs

Tie a few herbs in a square of thin cotton fabric. Hang under the hot tap for a super, refreshing soak.

Basil

Camomile

Lavender

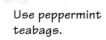

Use peppermint teabags.

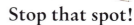

Ski-sticks make wacky patterns!

Sun care

Out in the sun, especially on the beach or skiing, your skin needs help! Protect your head, neck and hair with a hat or scarf. Apply stacks of suncream – select the right one for your skin type. Protect your eyes – especially when skiing.

Stop that spot!

Don't squeeze it, leave it! If you want, you could dab a little lemon juice on it using cotton wool.

2
SKILLS
FOR STYLE

KNITTING

You can become an ace knitter. You just need a little patience and help from a good knitter.
First you need to **'cast on'** some stitches.

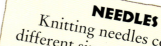

NEEDLES
Knitting needles come in different sizes. Begin with 4 or 5 mm ones and chunky wool.

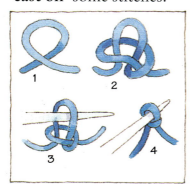

Make a slip knot. Put your left needle through the knot and tighten it.

Put right needle through loop from front to back. Wind the wool round right needle.

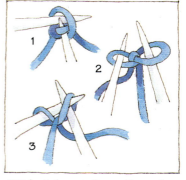

With right needle pull wool through first loop. Move this new loop onto left needle. Repeat for as many stitches as you need.

Super scrunchie

Cast on 22 stitches in glitter thread wool. Knit 195 rows. Cast off and finish scrunchie as on p.7.

Fab fringes

To finish off a scarf or to jazz up old jumpers add a fringe of tassels.

LEFT-HANDED TIP
If necessary, prop the book in front of a mirror to follow the pictures.

Wind wool loads of times round a small book. Cut along one side.

Take 2 lengths and fold in half. Pull loop through knitted stitch.

Use a crochet hook.

Thread ends through loop and tighten. Trim evenly.

Knit stitch

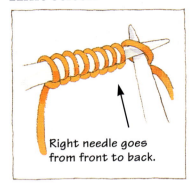

Right needle goes from front to back.

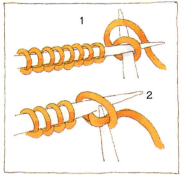

1
2

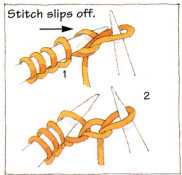

Stitch slips off.

1
2

Hold needle with cast-on stitches in left hand. Push right needle through first stitch.

Bring wool around right needle and pull it through first stitch.

Now you have loop on right needle, slip first stitch off left one. Continue with next stitch.

Casting off

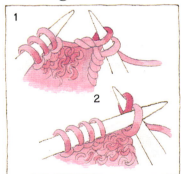

1
2

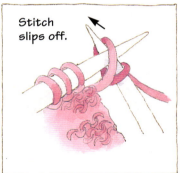

Stitch slips off.

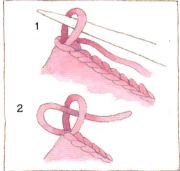

1
2

Knit 2 stitches. With left needle pick up first one and bring it over second one.

Let this stitch slip off both needles. Knit next stitch and bring previous stitch over it.

When 1 stitch is left, cut the wool and pull it through last stitch. Tighten to finish.

Knitted squares

Knit some squares and sew them together to make all kinds of things from bags to blankets.

Make a chunky plait for the strap.

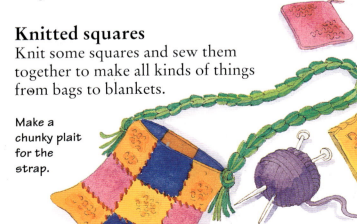

SEWING

Being able to sew is really useful. Then you don't need to ask anyone else to sew buttons back on, mend rips or take up hems.

THREADING TIP
It's easier if you make sure the thread is cut neatly, licked and pressed between your fingers!

Running stitch

Practise these stitches on scraps of fabric.

Hemming stitch

Knot thread before starting

Make sure stitches hardly show on 'right' side.

Handy hems

Pin hem to length you want. Sew in matching thread, using hemming stitch.

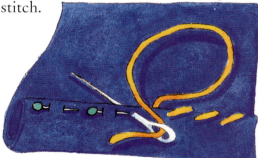

And to finish...

Knot thread as shown and pull thread tight. Snip off extra thread. Get a grown-up to help press new hem.

Fixing buttons

Make sure you place button so it goes through buttonhole. Start from behind the fabric and push the needle up through it and one of the holes in the button.

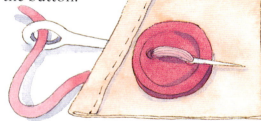

Push needle back through another hole and fabric. Continue until button feels secure.

Four-holed buttons can be sewn on in different ways.

LEFT-HANDED?
If you find scissors a bit tricky, you can get special ones for left-handers!

 14

Back stitch

Try to make stitches even.

Chain stitch

Hold loop with finger.

Cross stitch

Just 2 sideways stitches.

Practise and use other embroidery stitches – they look terrific on gloves, scarves, or T-shirts.

Rip repairs

Turn garment inside out. Pin ripped edges and use back stitch right across pins. Take pins out for a magic mend.

Put pins in sideways.

FUN FACT

Queen Elizabeth I of England never wore the same dress twice – but she had exact copies made so no one would think she was extravagant!

To make a nifty needlecase

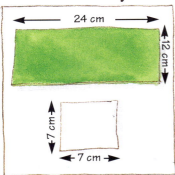

24 cm

12 cm

7 cm

7 cm

Use felt as it doesn't fray. Choose your own colours and cut felt to size.

Pin and sew the square inside the rectangle.

Decorate needlecase with buttons, sequins or try an embroidered design or initial.

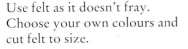

PAPIER MÂCHÉ

To make papier mâché

- 8 cups of water
- 4 cups of flour
- newspaper
- vaseline
- chosen mould e.g. plates, bowls, yoghurt pots, balloons.

Mix flour and water over a gentle heat, until smooth. Cool.

Tear the newspaper into strips.

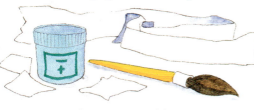

Coat your chosen mould with vaseline. Cover strips with paste and smooth them onto the mould. Cover mould completely with several layers. Leave to dry for 2 or 3 days in a warm, dry place. Then decorate and varnish (see opposite for ideas).

Check it isn't the best china first!

PASTE TIP
You can get paste in powder form from craft shops. Make sure it's non-toxic.

Bowls and balloons

These make great moulds but let your imagination wander. You can cover all kinds of everyday things! Or, make your own cardboard shapes (you don't have to remove the cardboard afterwards).

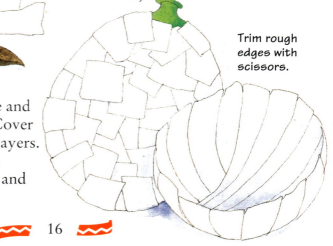

Trim rough edges with scissors.

Papier mâché pulp

This can be used just like modelling clay and is great for making beads (see p.18).

- 2 cups of flour
- 6 cups of water
- 2 or 3 newspapers torn into tiny squares.

Mix flour and water until smooth. Stir in the newspaper and let it stand for 2-3 hours.

As you mould it into shapes squeeze out excess water.

Fab finishes

- Paint finished objects with white emulsion to use as a background.
- Use poster paints or glitter paint.
- Use fine fabric like silk or coloured tissue paper as a smashing final layer.
- Glue on seeds, shells, pasta in patterns before painting.
- Varnish when paint is dry but remember it doesn't make it waterproof!

FUN FACT
1700-year-old Chinese warrior masks made from papier mâché still survive today!

Try some animals.

Reuse egg cartons.

Party masks

Use a balloon covered in vaseline. Paste about 5 layers on half of it. When dry, take out or pop balloon. Trim edges and cut holes for eyes.

Make holes and thread with elastic.

Paint on features – animal or human.

JEWELLERY

It's fun to make your own and great for gifts too! You could even get together with friends to sell what you make at your next school fair.

Brill bangles

Make a cardboard band to fit your wrist or cut down a cardboard tube. Wind papier mâché strips (see p.16) round it. Dry and then paint and varnish.

(see p.16)

Answers on inside back cover

JEWELLERY QUIZ

1 Is it true that the Victorians used to set locks of hair into jewellery?
2 Which of the following jewellery stones is made of fossilized tree sap: sapphire, amber, garnet?

(Answers on inside back cover)

Thread onto elastic when dry.

Papier mâché beads

Make up pulp as on p.17. Cover a knitting needle with vaseline.

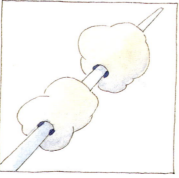

Take a small dollop of pulp and press around knitting needle into required shape.

Potato makes a good drying stand.

Dry for 4-5 days. Take off needle and let the middle dry for a day. Paint and varnish.

Junk jewellery

Be inspired to recycle rubbish! Old buttons, coloured paper-clips, feathers, corks and bits of foil can all be used for fab and unusual jewellery.

Clip-on earring

Brooch pin

The metal bits, like brooch pins, for making jewellery are called *findings*. They're available in craft shops if you get seriously into it!

Earring hook

Screw fitting

EAR TIP
Only have your ears pierced by someone qualified to do it. Doing it yourself could lead to a nasty infection.

Crazy earrings

Glue on a doll's-house plate, knife and fork or other miniature things to a square of painted card. You can make each earring different! You will need clip-on earring findings on the backs of these.

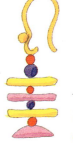
Buttons   Telephone wire   Silver foil
(Remove thin wires from outer casing.)

Clever clay

You can get self-hardening clay from craft shops. It comes in brilliant colours and you just bake it in the oven according to the instructions on the pack.

Make a rabbit or fish brooch from clay pieces. Take care when cutting.

You'll need brooch pins to glue on the back of these.

Try and make an abstract design brooch.

Wool bracelet

Use scraps of wool to make a plaited wristband (see p.4). Take 6 strands and plait 2 at a time.

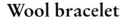

CLOTHES

You don't need to spend loads of money to create your own funky style in clothes.

Designer T-shirts

Buy an old T-shirt from a jumble sale or charity shop and use fabric paints to transform it. It doesn't have to be a pattern or picture – try a slogan like 'Save the Planet'!

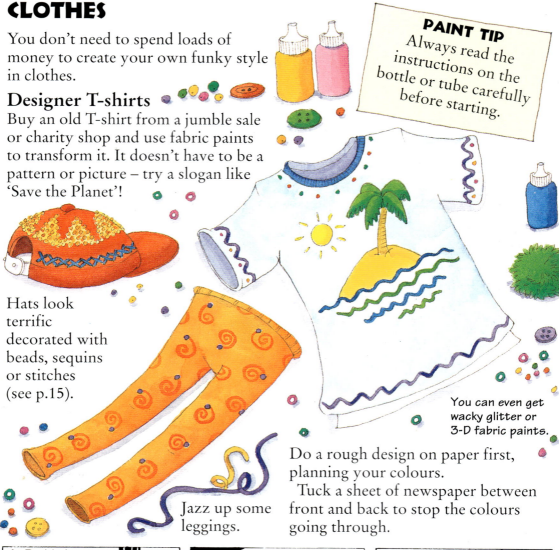

Hats look terrific decorated with beads, sequins or stitches (see p.15).

PAINT TIP
Always read the instructions on the bottle or tube carefully before starting.

You can even get wacky glitter or 3-D fabric paints.

Jazz up some leggings.

Do a rough design on paper first, planning your colours.

Tuck a sheet of newspaper between front and back to stop the colours going through.

At Beth's house –

ER, BETH, WHAT ARE YOU LOOKING FOR IN THAT PILE OF OLD STUFF?

THIS...NO...UM... YEAH, THIS'LL DO.

THIS OLD KNITTED WAISTCOAT WILL LOOK GREAT WHEN I'VE PUT A FRINGE ON IT.

A few days later –

HEY, THAT LOOKS DEAD COOL BETH. WILL YOU DO ONE FOR ME?

To make a pompom

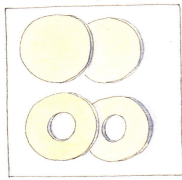

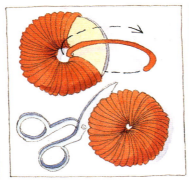

Trim with scissors.

Cut out 2 circles of card. Cut a small circle in the middle of each one.

Put the circles together and wind wool round them until the hole has gone. Cut between the 2 circles.

Tie some wool tightly between the circles. Cut and gently remove card and fluff up pompom.

Hat and scarf magic

Brighten up a woollen scarf or hat with tassels (see p.12) or pompoms. Use plaited wool to complete a pompom if you want it to dangle.

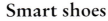

Tassels

Smart shoes

You can even use fabric paints on canvas shoes. Stuff them with newspaper first.
  They're great for gifts!

Long cotton scarves look fun tied as hairbands or belts.

Use jazzy coloured laces too.

YOUR ROOM

Whether you have a big or small room or even if you are sharing, you can still make your own special space. Give your bed a style by making some cushions in your favourite colours. Decorate them with fabric paints, felt cut-outs, embroidery stitches or pompoms!

Make a sign for your bedroom door.

Personal pinboard

If you haven't got a pinboard make one from insulation board or cork. It's wonderful for keeping all your favourite photos and postcards and all those other things you collect!

Attach a handy pencil and note-pad to your pinboard.

Design a special border that says something about you, maybe an animal border if you love animals.

SOCKS

LETTERS

Cover and decorate shoe boxes to store all those bits and pieces. It'll stop your mum coming into your room and moving all your stuff around!

STAYING HEALTHY

EAT WELL

To stay healthy you need to eat a balanced diet.

It's OK to eat burgers and chips and cakes and biscuits occasionally – but make sure that's not all you eat!

CUT DOWN ON FAST FOOD!

GOOD TO EAT!

Keep teeth healthy

Try having a sweet day once a week. If you do eat sweets, it's best to eat them all at once and then have a good rinse with water.

Brush your teeth morning and night.

Scrummy snacks

Instead of crisps and biscuits or sweets, try snacking on fresh fruit or a few nuts.

Visit your dentist twice a year.

Dried fruit is very good for you but not so good for your teeth! Clean your teeth as soon as you can after eating it.

GNASHER NEWS
1 The oldest false teeth ever found are about 2700 years old!
2 Babies aren't usually born with teeth but one was born recently with 12!

SUPERMARKET TIP
Look at the lists of ingredients on tins and packets – you'll be amazed at how many 'savoury' things include sugar!

Lunch-box treats

Help out and make your own lunch for school or an outing or picnic. Can you help with shopping too, so you plan ahead?

Set the alarm clock a little earlier.

Pitta bread stuffed with salad, cold chicken or cheese
Carrot
Apple
Orange juice

Roll with cream cheese, apple slices and lettuce
Celery sticks
Box of raisins
Pear, and grape juice

Rice salad (with yellow pepper and raisins)
Cheese
Peanuts
Banana, and pineapple juice

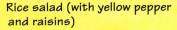

Cream cheese and tuna sandwich
Peanut butter and banana sandwich
Orange
Apple juice

Yellow Peril!

Recycle old plastic containers. Make sure they're watertight and the lids are on firmly.

DRINKS
Drink pure fruit juices or water. Avoid sugary fizzy drinks!

COOK'S CORNER

Cooking is great fun – as long as you take care with knives and hot stoves or ovens. Ask if you can prepare a meal once a week for your family, or treat your friends.

REMEMBER
Wash your hands before you start cooking and tie on an apron!

Chopping vegetables

Use a sharp knife and wooden board. Slice or cut in half and half again and again until they are the size you want.

Washing lettuce

Cut off the stalk and any yellow leaves. Wash several times in fresh water, shake and pat dry in a clean cloth.

Wash fresh fruit and veg before cooking and eating.

Keep pets off work surfaces!

Clear up after cooking and wash up in hot soapy water. Rinse before drying.

Cooking pasta

1 Fill a large saucepan with water and 2 teaspoons of salt. Bring to the boil (that's when it bubbles).
2 Add pasta. Use about 100 g per person for a big meal. Stir once. Lower heat to gentle bubbling. Check the packet for cooking time. Test a little piece first.
3 Drain into colander and serve immediately.

Salad dressing

salt   pepper

2 tablespoons oil   1 teaspoon vinegar

At school –

...AND I COULDN'T LIVE WITHOUT MY MUM'S SHEPHERD'S PIE.

I COULDN'T BE VEGGY LIKE YOU BETH, I LOVE MY BACON SARNIES!

WELL, I JUST DON'T LIKE EATING ANIMALS BUT I EAT LOADS OF CHEESE AND BEANS.

Vegetarians don't eat meat – sometimes for religious reasons, or because they don't like animals being killed.

Sauce for pasta (for 2)
Try cooking this delicious pasta sauce. It's meat-free, so OK for vegetarians too.

- 1 small onion, chopped
- 1 carrot, chopped
- 200 g tin of tomatoes
- 50 g red lentils, washed (in sieve)
- Olive or vegetable oil
- Pinch of mixed herbs
- Salt and pepper to taste

VEGGY TIP
Before going to a friend's house to eat, don't forget to mention that you're vegetarian and don't eat meat!

Serve on cooked pasta.

HALF-BAKED
Can you complete the top half of these foodie words?

YOGHURT

SANDWICH

RECIPE

(Answers on inside back cover)

Serve with a green salad and a glass of milk.

Fry the onion and carrot gently in the oil until soft.

Add tin of tomatoes, lentils, herbs, salt and pepper. Let it bubble.

Lower heat and simmer for 20 minutes. Add a little water if it's too thick.

 27

GO GREEN

Help our planet to feel great too! Here are a few suggestions. Remember every little helps.

DON'T JUST BIN IT!

RECYCLE IT!

Take bottles, paper and aluminium cans to be recycled.

$ £ $
You can make extra money for a charity by selling cans.

Try and reuse plastic and packaging. Keep a collection of bits and pieces for collages or jewellery (see p.19).

Adopt an animal

If you have some spare pocket money or have raised some money you could adopt an animal in danger.

Useful addresses: inside back cover.

Sort out your old clothes and toys regularly. Can you give them to someone younger, or take them to a hospital or charity shop?

NEED A BAG!
Reuse carrier bags or just get a sturdy bag instead.

YUK!
Last but not least! Always clean up after your dog.

Tree check

Trees are homes and food to birds, animals and insects.

Green trees pump oxygen into the air

In dry weather, a bucket of water can save a tree.

Collect seeds to grow seedlings and plant a tree.

Compost

Turn vegetable peelings into compost. Drill holes in an old dustbin. Buy worms (called *brandlings*) from a fishing shop. Put them in the bin with the peelings.

Pest control

Wiggly worms are soil savers! They make soil when they digest their food and their tunnels bring air and water to the soil.

SAVE US !

Hedgehogs are one of nature's own pest controllers – they eat slugs and caterpillars.

A 5-POINT PLAN
What you can do!

1 Pick up litter.
2 Save water. Turn off the tap while you're cleaning your teeth.
3 Recycle rubbish.
4 Walk or go by bike or bus to reduce pollution.
5 Save electricity. Turn off the lights when you leave a room.

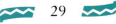

GET FIT

Eating well is only one side of staying healthy. You also need to keep your body tuned up and take regular exercise.

FIT FACT

For exercise to do any good, you need to get a bit out of breath!

SPORTS QUIZ

1 How often are the Olympic Games held?
2 How many sports are there in a pentathlon event?
3 What is a racing crawl?

(Answers on inside back cover)

Bike it!

Wear a helmet and reflective strips.

Make sure your brakes work.

Whether you've a cool cycle or an old banger, bikes are brilliant for fitness.

Design a fitness circuit or obstacle race

– in your garden, park or even in a room. Here are some ideas: 20 skips, running 100 steps on the spot, touching your toes 10 times, sitting down and standing up 10 times. *Breathless?!!*

Skipping

It's a great way to exercise. You can do it almost anywhere and you don't need much special equipment.

You could organize a sponsored 'skip in' – skipping in non-stop relays with your friends – to raise money for charity and get fit too!

TURN ME OFF!

Just watch your favourite television programmes. Don't get stuck in front of the telly!

YOGA

What's that?

It's a form of exercise many thousands of years old. The movements are slow and gentle and really relaxing.

Here is Beth demonstrating 3 yoga 'postures'. You could look up some more at the library. Try a few minutes after a hard day at school!

CARE TIP
With all exercise, you might feel a bit stiff, especially at first. But remember, if any exercise really hurts, STOP!

Beth at home –

HEAD ROLLS FIRST

MM, I'M BREATHING DEEPLY. I FEEL NICE AND RELAXED!

DROP MY HEAD FORWARD AND ROLL RIGHT ROUND SLOWLY.

NOW ROLL IT BACK THE OTHER WAY– COO, I MUST BE STIFF IT'S MAKING A CLICKY NOISE!

Next day –

RIGHT, JENNY, ALWAYS BREATHE DEEPLY TO START WITH. SIT BACK ON YOUR HEELS.

OPEN YOUR EYES AND MOUTH AS WIDE AS POSSIBLE AND SLOWLY STICK YOUR TONGUE OUT.

WHAT!

I HOPE NO ONE COMES IN!

NOW RELAX.

I CAN SEE WHY IT'S CALLED 'THE LION'!

Getting more expert –

OK YOU TWO WE'LL TRY BALANCING ON ONE LEG. IT'S CALLED 'THE TREE'.

STAND UP AS STRAIGHT AS POSSIBLE. KEEP UP YOUR DEEP BREATHING!

IT'S SIMPLE!

HUH! IT'S OK FOR YOU YOU'VE BEEN PRACTISING!

INDEX

Published by b small publishing
Pinewood, 3a Coombe Ridings, Kingston-upon-Thames, Surrey KT2 7JT
© b small publishing, 1994
3 4 5
All rights reserved.
Design: Lone Morton *Editorial*: Catherine Bruzzone and Susan Martineau *Production*: Grahame Griffiths
No reproduction, copy or transmission of this publication may be made without written permission.
No part of this publication may be reproduced, stored in a retrieval system, or transmitted in any form or by any means,
electronic, mechanical, photocopying, recording or otherwise, without the prior permission of the publisher.
Colour reproduction: Next Graphic Ltd, Hong Kong.
Printed in Italy by Isabel Litografia srl
ISBN 1 874735 16 6
British Library Cataloguing-in-Publication Data. A catalogue record for this book is available from the British Library.